CHRISTMAS
in
Stained Glass
II

by Carolyn Kyle

CKE Publications
Olympia, Washington

Acknowledgements

In the heat of summer, with not a jingle bell within sight or sound, Chuck Berets fabricated most of the projects in this book. Those who know Chuck will understand his sacrifice when they equate it to how many evenings of fishing he has given up.

Chuck's daughter, Tana Berets, was his able assistant in the foiling department. Our good friends Jan Schrader, Ken Bubnick, and Dave Gagne also helped out by building projects. Thank you all.

I'd also like to give special thanks to Karen Hayes, who kindly allowed us to photograph her version of the nativity scene.

Carolyn Kyle

Photography: Russ Runyan, Capital Photo Lab, Olympia, Washington
Consultation: Colony Glass Works, Olympia, Washington

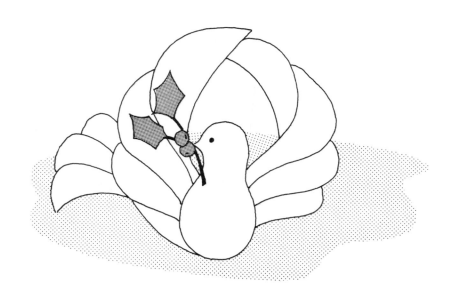

DISTRIBUTION:

CKE PUBLICATIONS
2840-E Black Lake Blvd.
Olympia, WA 98502
Tel: (206) 352-4427
Fax: (206) 943-3978

CKE PUBLICATIONS EUROPE
Tichelbrink 68\ Postfach 3021
D-4972 Löhne-Gohfeld
West Germany
Telfon: 05731-83307
Fax: 05731-82840

TREE ORNAMENTS

Christmas is music

TREE ORNAMENTS

Christmas is treats

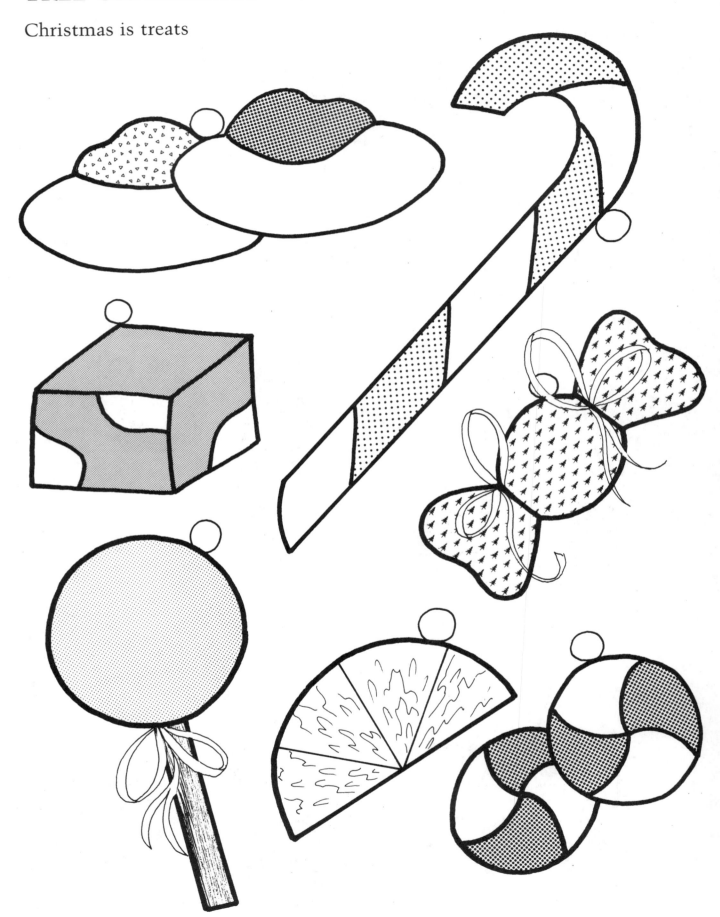

TREE ORNAMENTS

Christmas is treasures

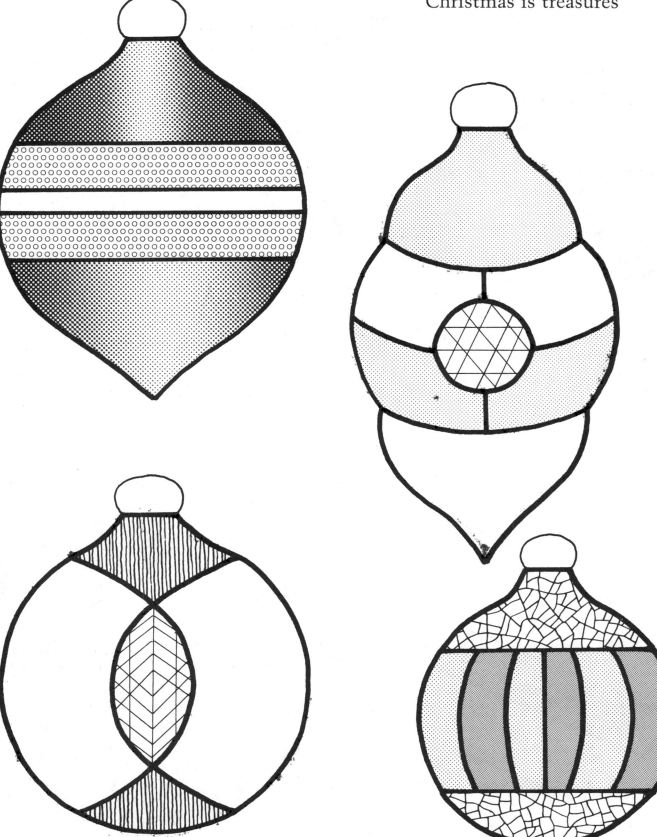

Hang these tree ornaments in front of lights on your tree.

TREE ORNAMENTS

Christmas is children

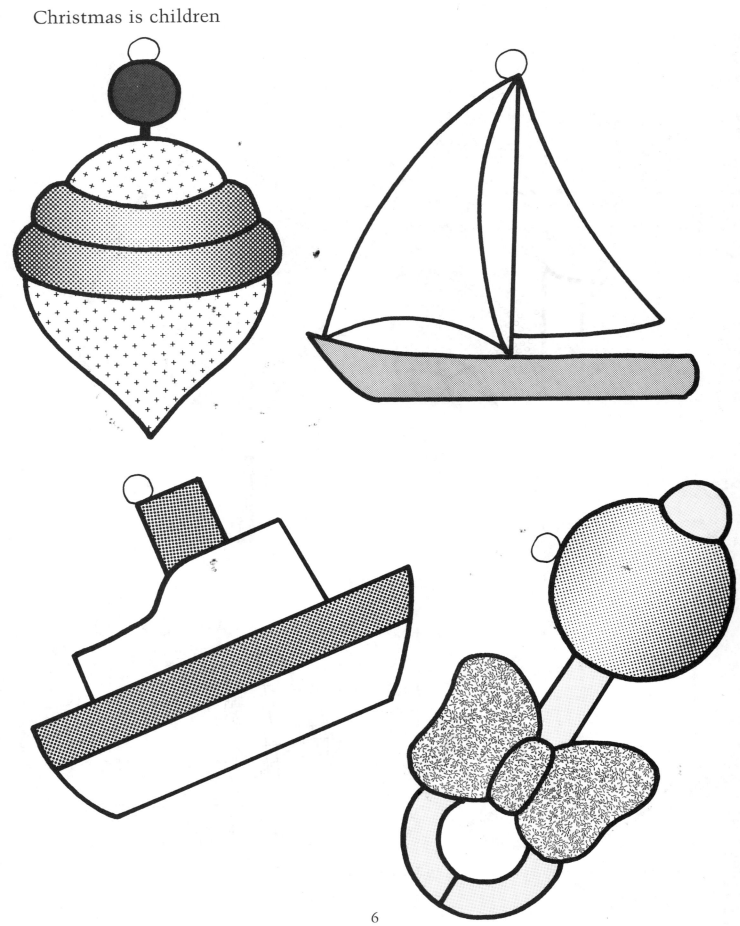

TREE ORNAMENTS

Christmas is toys

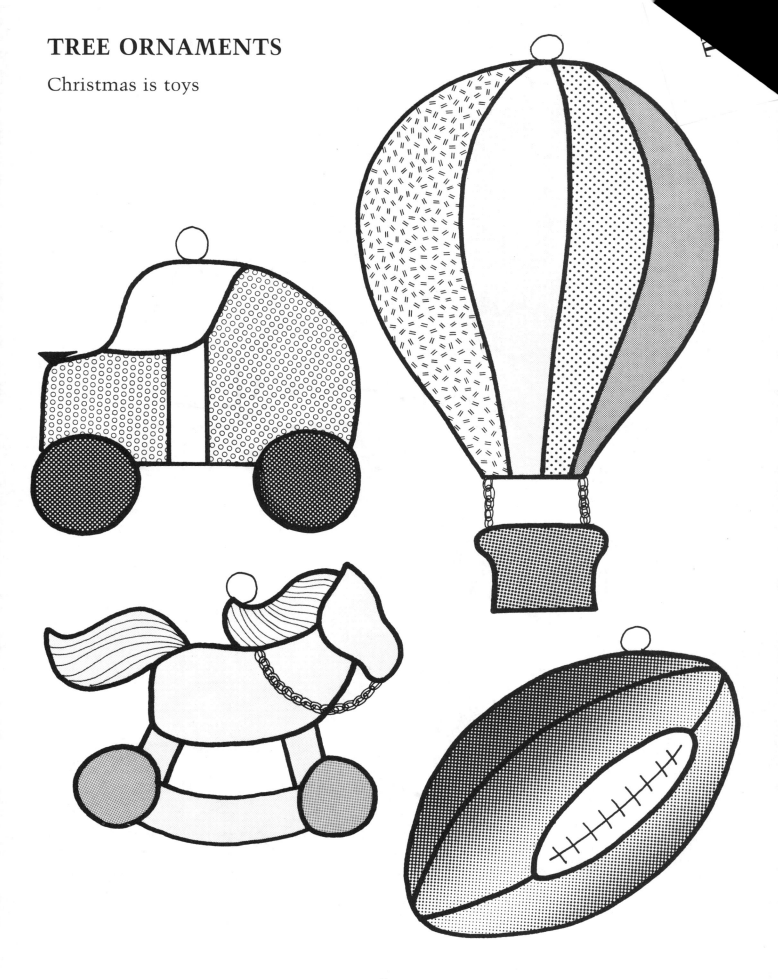

Christmas is warmth

Hang these tree ornaments
in front of lights
on your tree.

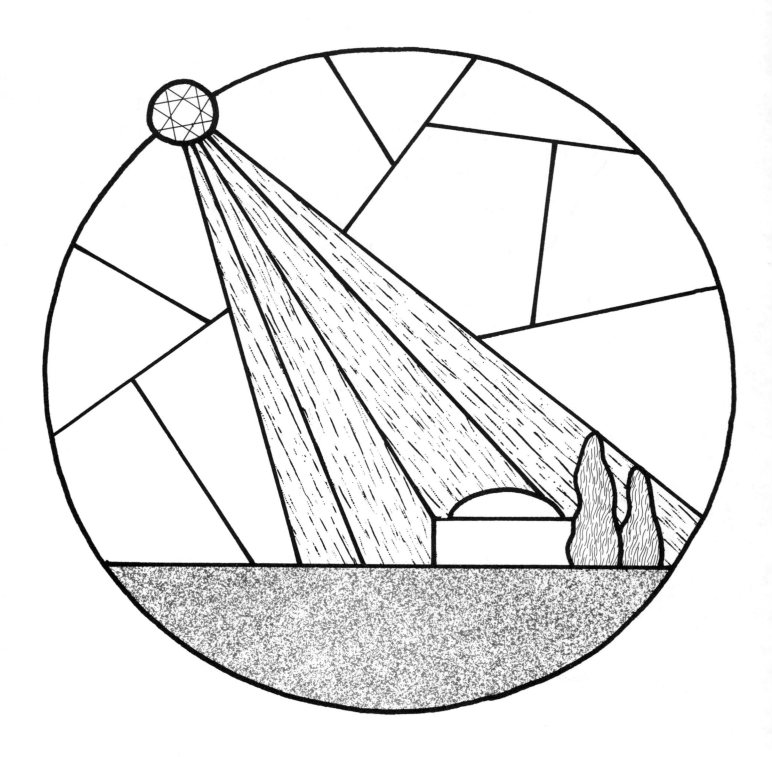

CHRISTMAS IS LOVE

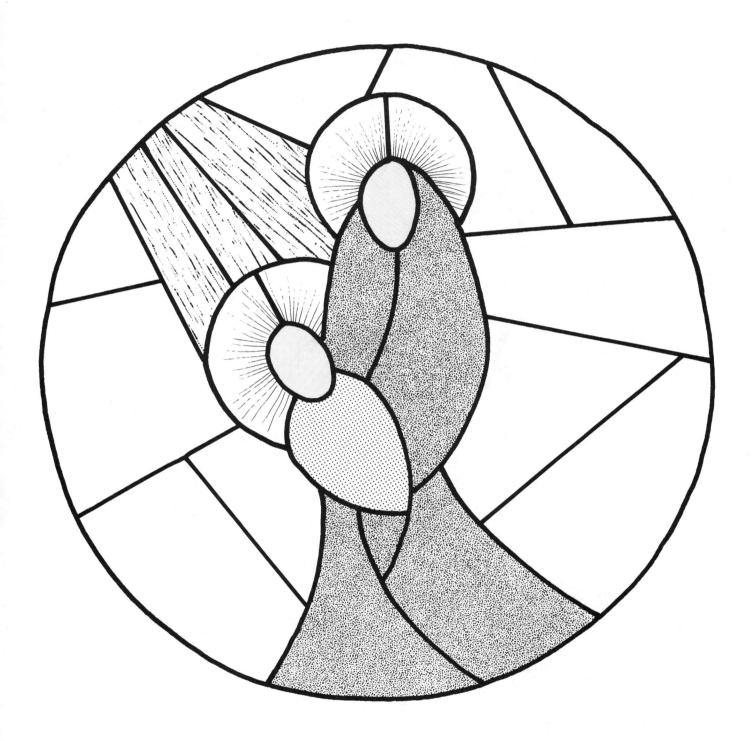

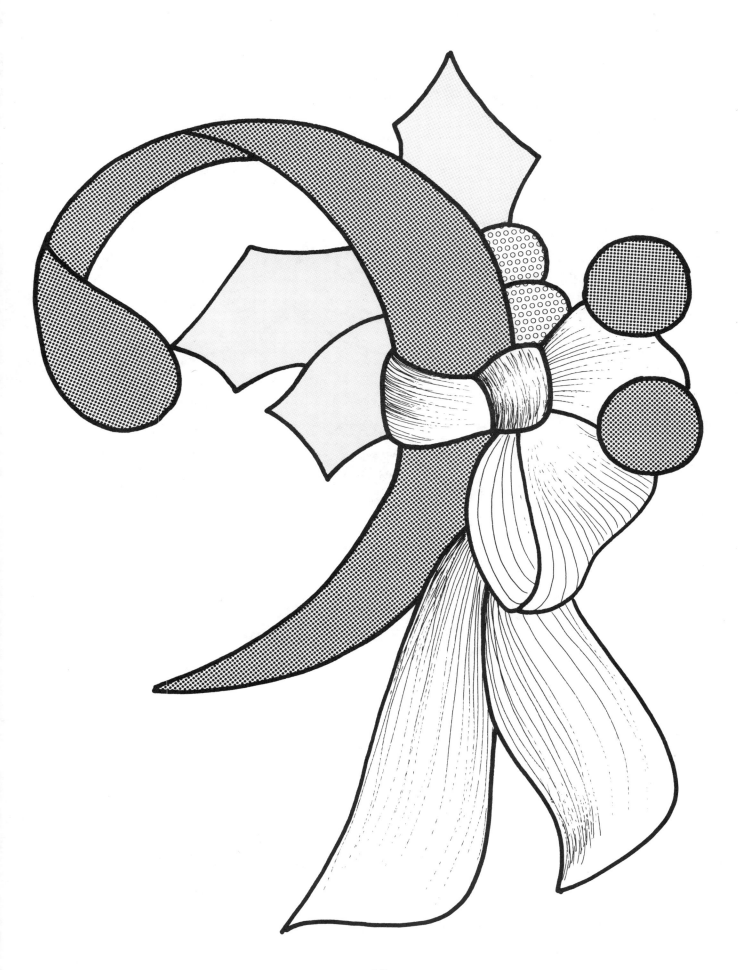

HANGING OR TABLE DECORATION

Follow the dotted line to make the tabletop version. See pages 26 and 57 for ways to make this project stand by itself.

HANGING OR TABLE DECORATION

See pages 26 and 57
for ways to make
this project stand
by itself.

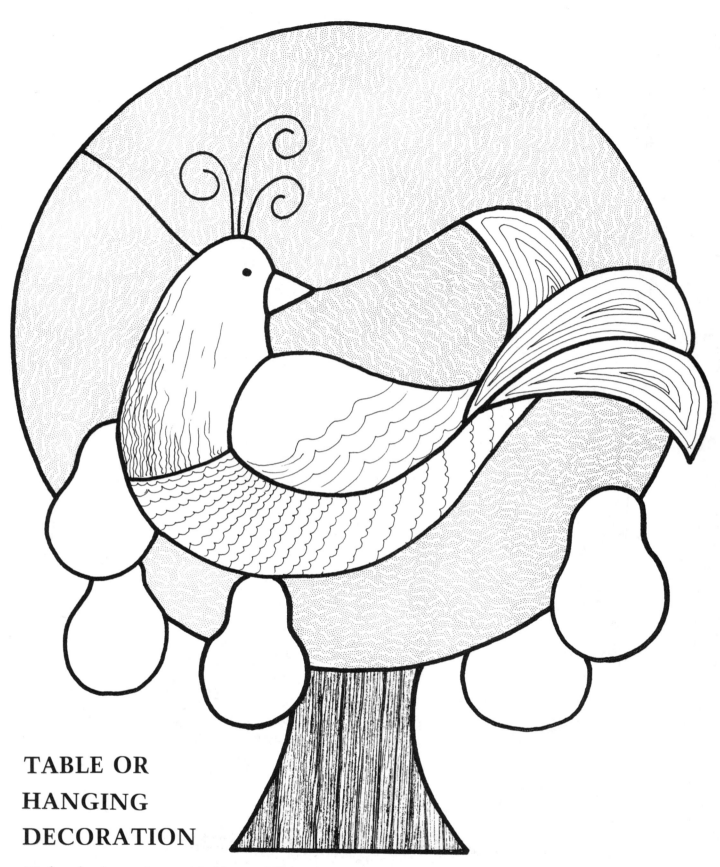

TABLE OR
HANGING
DECORATION

Make the base about 6 inches wide and center the tree trunk in the middle. Bend wires and attach them to the partridge's head after the project is assembled. See pages 26 and 57 for ways to make this project stand by itself.

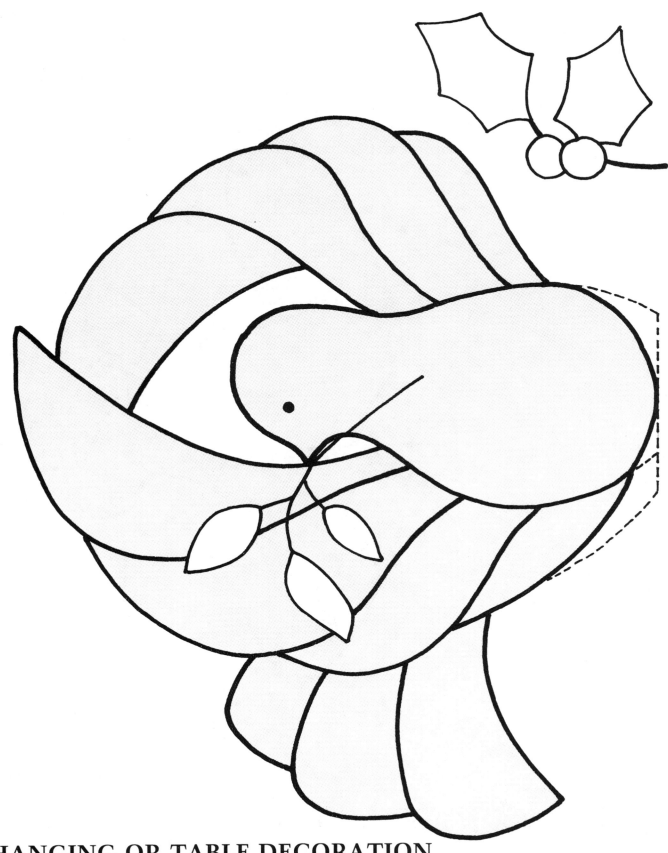

HANGING OR TABLE DECORATION

Make the olive branch or holly sprig separately, then overlay it on the finished dove and lightly tack it in place. Follow the dotted lines to make a tabletop version. See pages 26 and 57 for ways to make the project stand by itself.

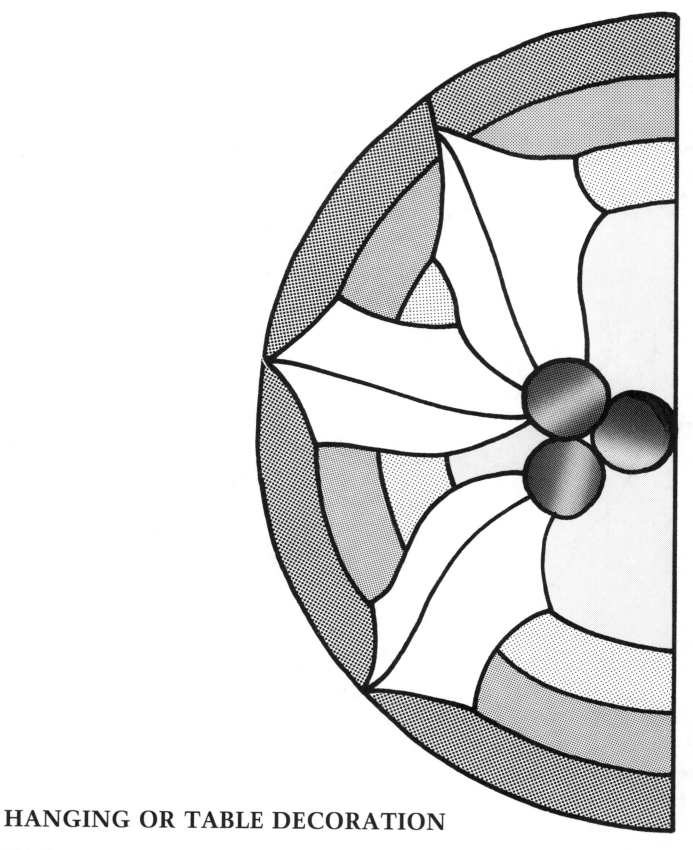

HANGING OR TABLE DECORATION

This decoration is attractive with a votive candle or tall candles behind it. Or, enclose it in an envelope with the message "Wishing you a rainbow of Christmas Cheer" for a permanent Christmas card remembrance. See pages 26 and 57 for ways to make the project stand by itself.

HANGING OR TABLE DECORATION

A votive candle behind this decoration would be attractive. See pages 26 and 57 for ways to make the project stand by itself.

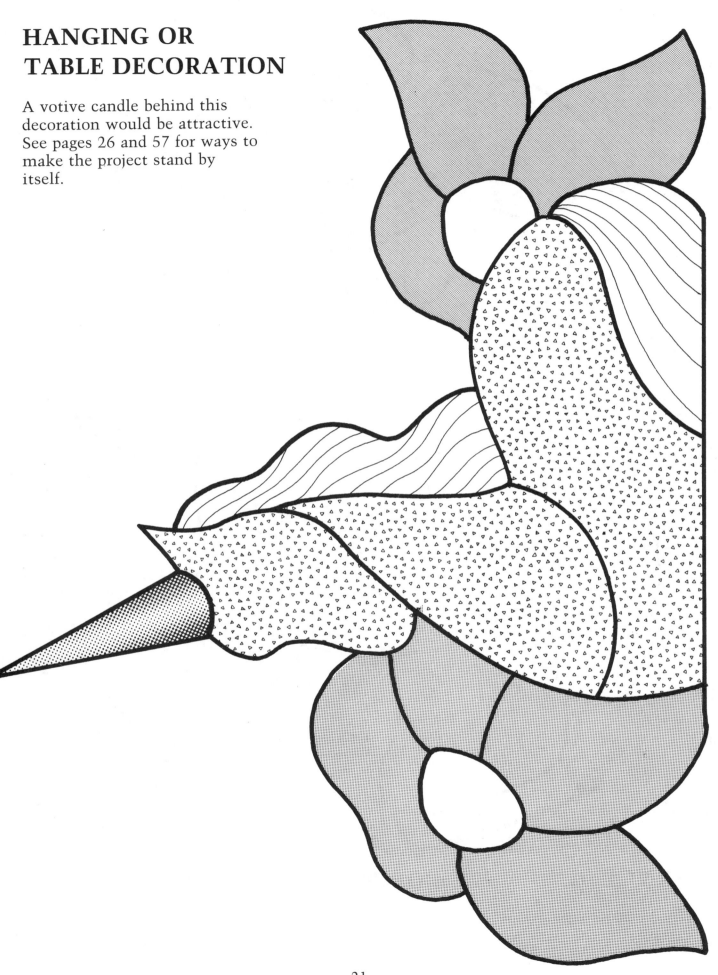

21

HANGING OR TABLE DECORATION

Tilt the standing snowboy slightly to the right and solder both ice skates to the glass base. See pages 26 and 57 for ways to make the project stand by itself.

HANGING OR TABLE DECORATIONS

The birdie will balance on ice skates by bending one skate forward and the other backward. See pages 26 and 57 for ways to make the snowgirl stand.

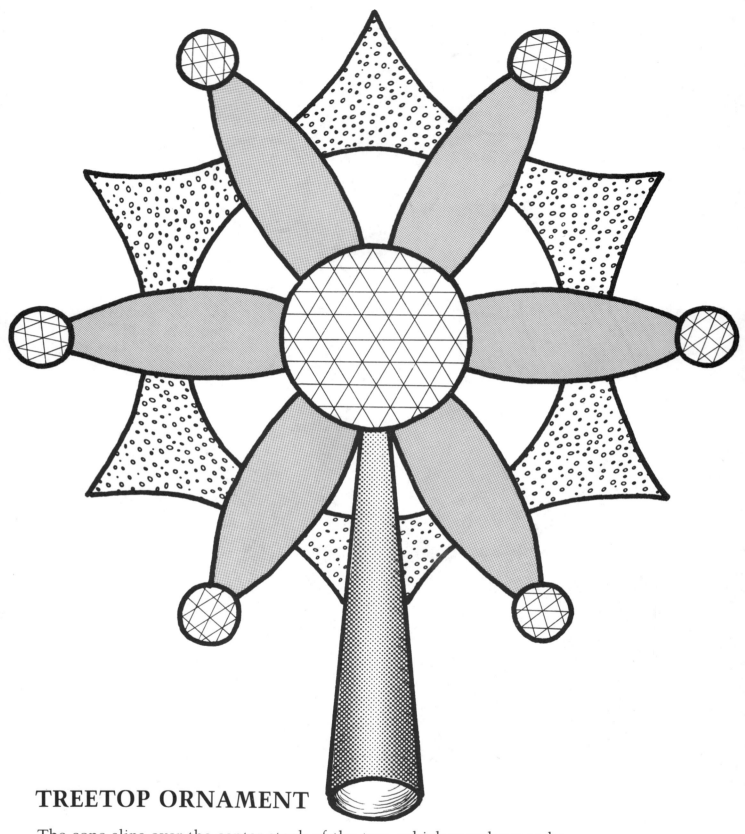

TREETOP ORNAMENT

The cone slips over the center stock of the tree, which may have to be trimmed slightly. To hold a Christmas light in place behind the ornament, solder a short length or wire to the back, just under the center jewel. Place the string of tree lights so that one of the lights will be behind the ornament. Then wrap the wire on the back or the ornament loosely around the base of the light. See page 26 for instructions on how to make and attach the cone base. Any pretty glass may be substituted for jewels.

24

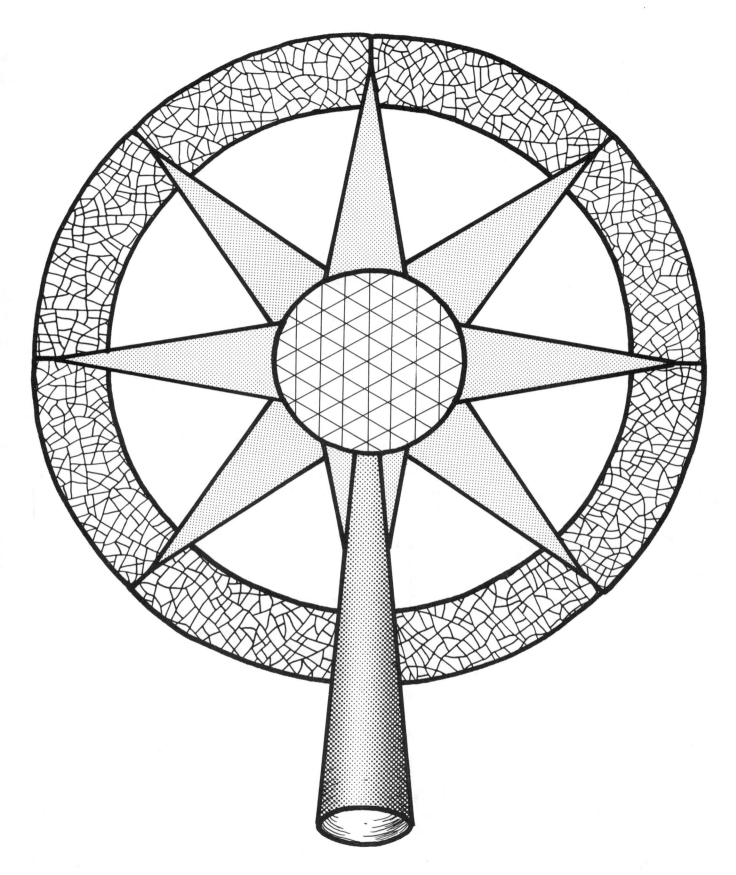

TREETOP ORNAMENT

See page 26 for instructions on how to make and attach the
cone base. Use any pretty glass as a substitute for the jewel.

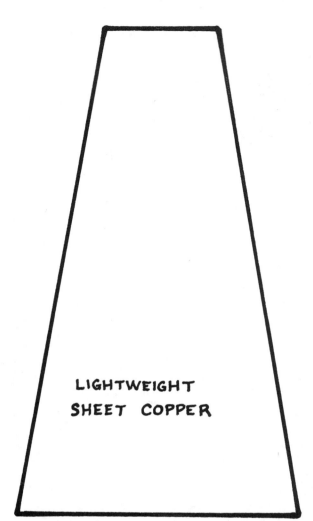

LIGHTWEIGHT
SHEET COPPER

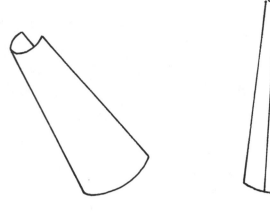

CONE FOR TREETOP ORNAMENT

Cut this shape from lightweight sheet copper. (Hobby supply stores should have sheet copper if stained glass supply stores don't.) Roll the copper shape to form a long tube as shown, overlapping the edges slightly. Flux and solder the seam. Tin the entire outer surface of the cone with solder for added strength. Solder the shape securely in place in the ornament, squeezing the shape if necessary for fit.

TABLE DECORATION BASE TO HOLD VOTIVE CANDLE

Cut this shape or a larger one from mirror. Wrap with foil and solder the project along the straight edge at about 85 degrees (at a very slight backward tilt). Brace if necessary with wire or braising rod.

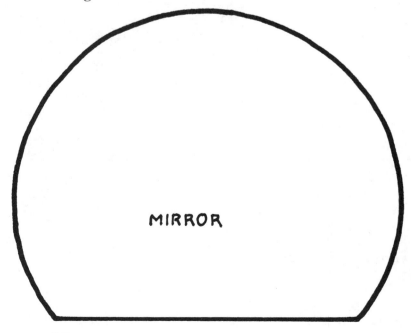

MIRROR

BACK VIEW

HANGING DECORATION OR TREETOP ORNAMENT

For the halo, twist two strands of lightweight copper wire together; tin, bend into shape, and solder in place on the assembled angel.

For the lace (optional), use fine chain, such as is used in glass boxes. Loop the chain and solder it lightly only where it touches the hems.

For the treetop ornament version, see page 26 for instructions on how to make the cone base; however, lengthen the cone to 6½ inches. Solder the cone to the back of the finished angel with 1½ inches of cone extending down beyond the hem of the dress.

HANGING OR TABLE DECORATION
OR A TREETOP ORNAMENT

Follow the dotted line to make the tabletop version. See pages 26 and 57 for ways to make the project stand by itself.

To make a treetop ornament, see page 26 for instructions on making a cone base, but lengthen it to 7½ inches. Solder the cone to the back of the ornament with 1½ inches of the cone extending down beyond the hem of the dress.

HANGING OR TABLE DECORATION OR TREETOP ORNAMENT

Use bevel, jewel, or yellow glass for the star. Use heavy copper wire for the staff and solder it in place last.

Follow the dotted line to make a tabletop version. For a tree ornament version, make a copper cone 8 inches long, solder it in back of the ornament with 1½ inches extending beyond the bottom center.

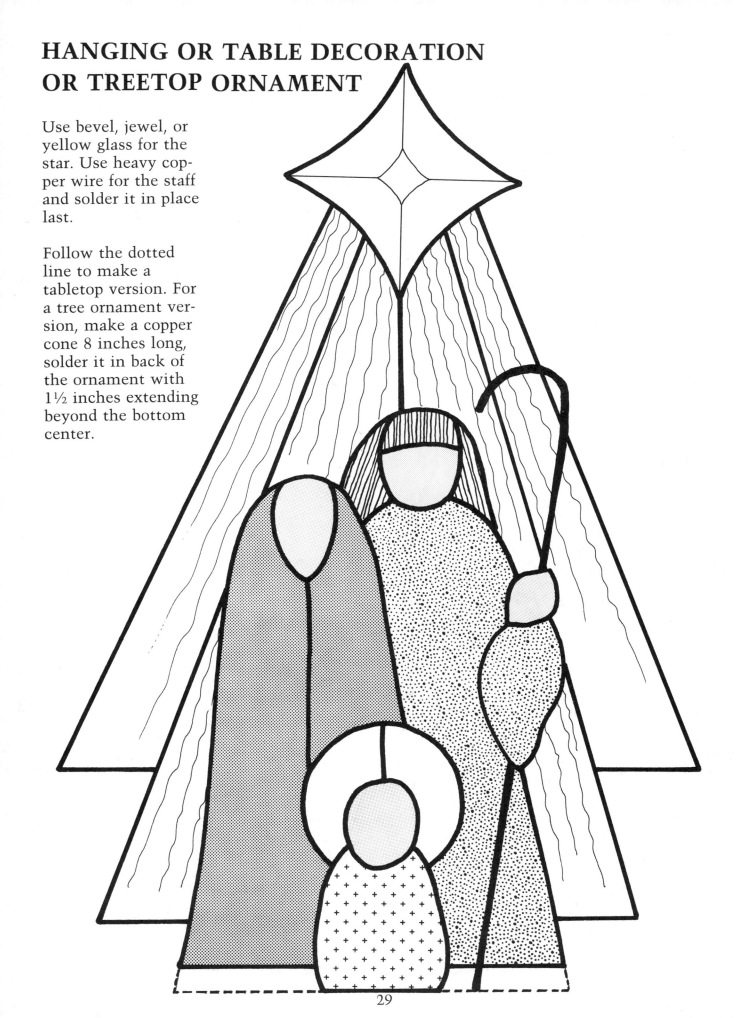

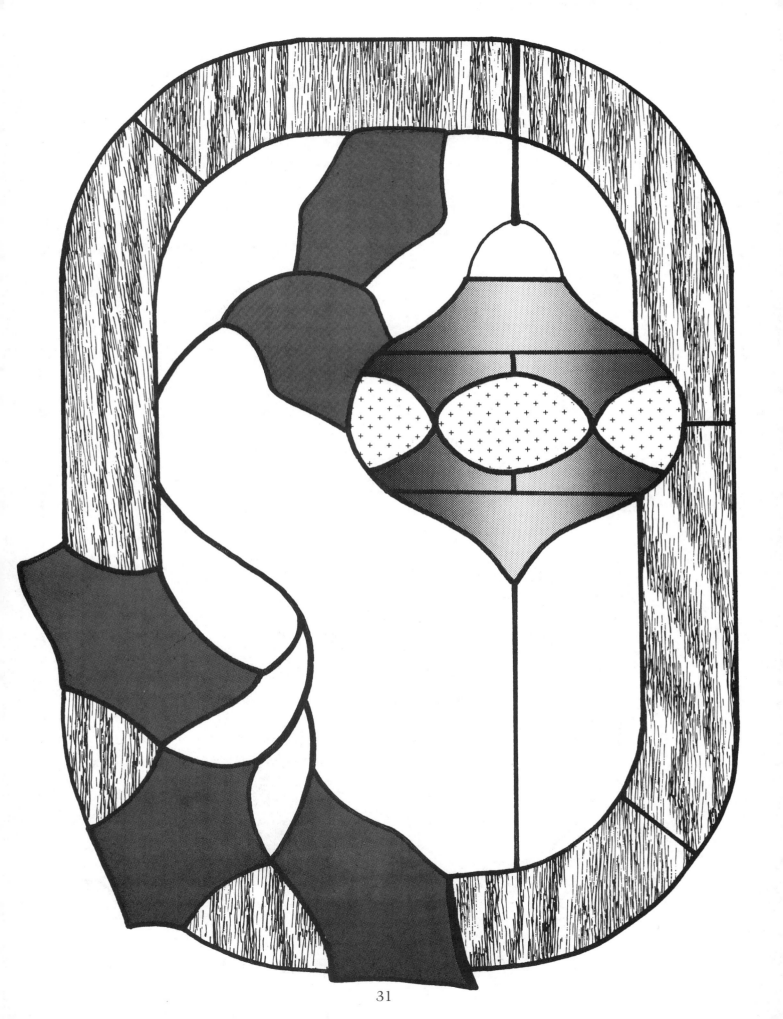

31

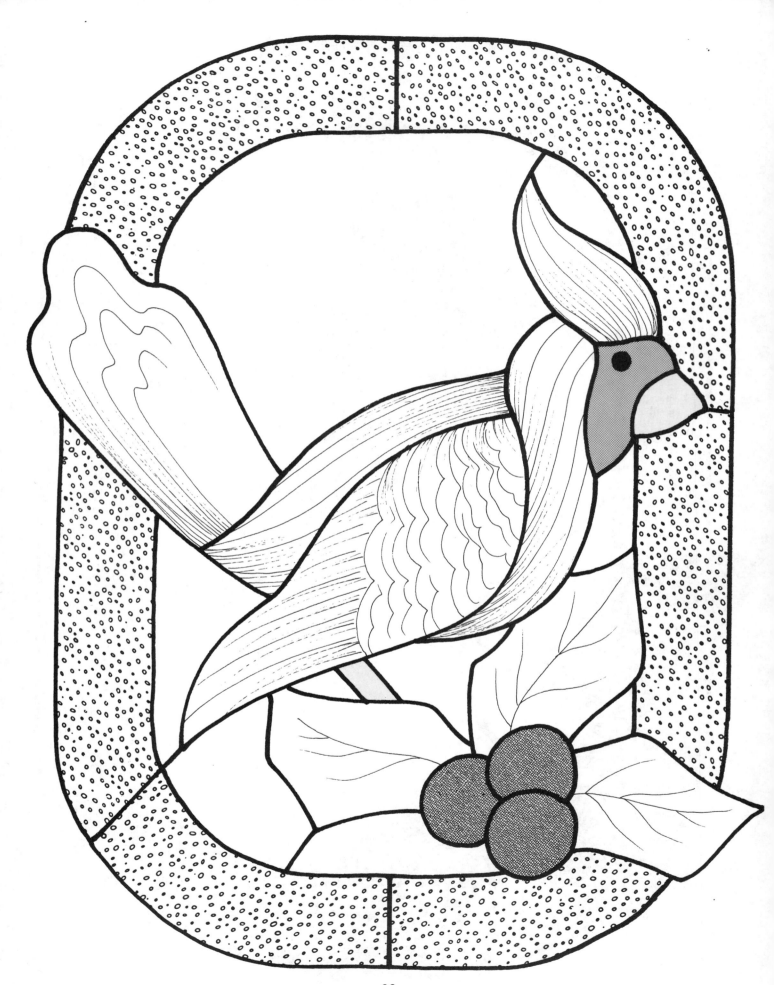

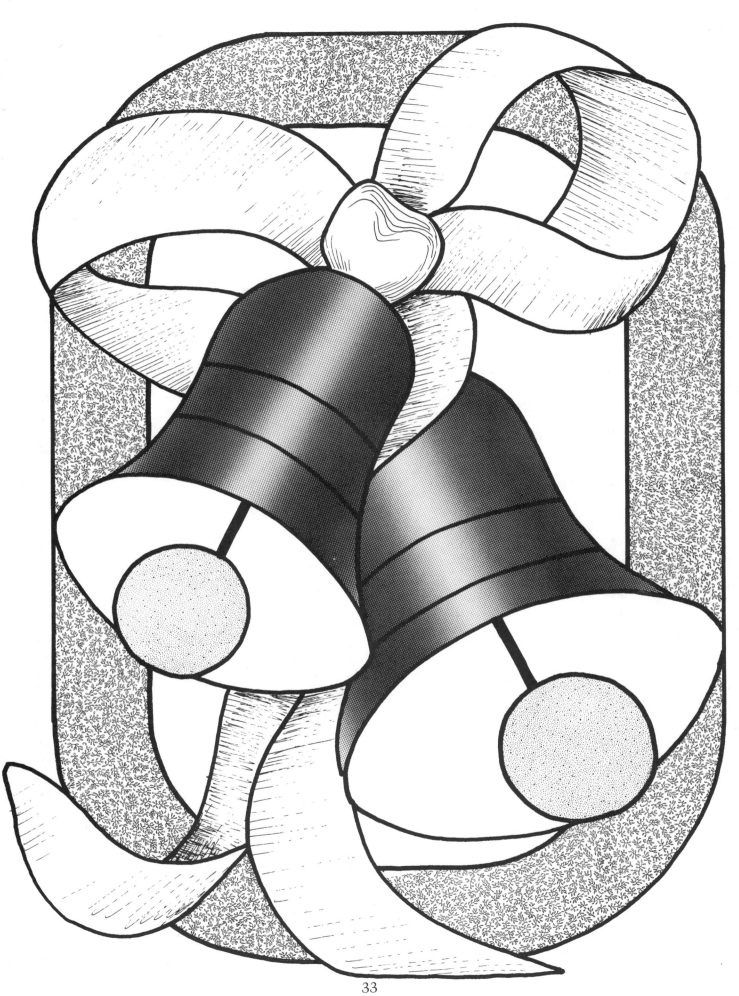

33

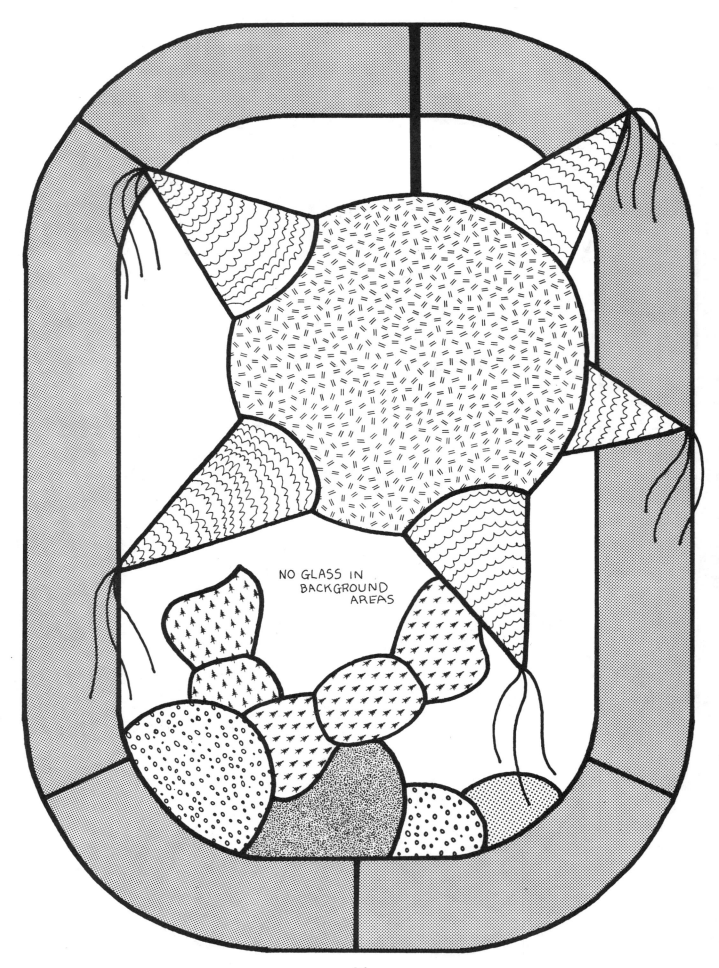

NO GLASS IN
BACKGROUND
AREAS

36

THE CHRISTMAS MINI-PANEL

—a nice size for gifts

These little Christmas panels will say "Seasons Greetings" for you year after year.

DESIGN YOUR OWN MINI-PANEL

Trace your favorite suncatcher pattern or patterns (Christmas or otherwise) inside this frame. A design that spills over the frame is especially interesting. Any open space between the suncatcher and the frame can be left open or be filled in with background glass.

If glass is to fill in the background, examine the background for cutability. Points or extreme arcs must have lines connected to them as illustrated. Feel free to put in, take out, or change any lines or shapes. Your originality will be a bonus.

MAKE SUNCATCHERS

Remove the borders and backgrounds from mini-panel designs on pages 30 through 36 for a fresh group of Christmas suncatchers.

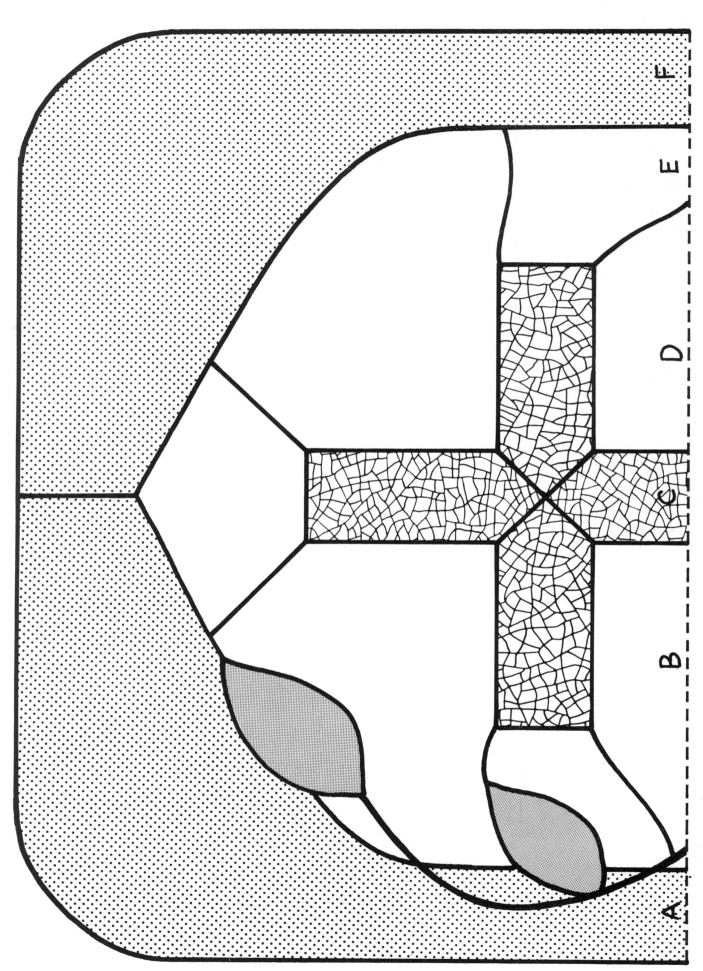

38

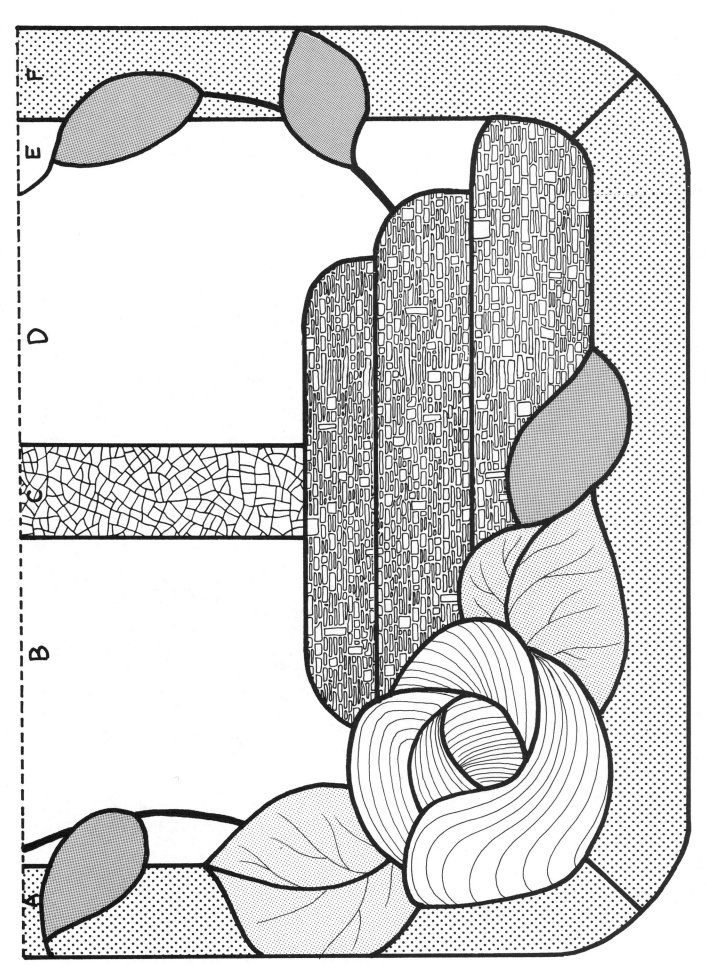

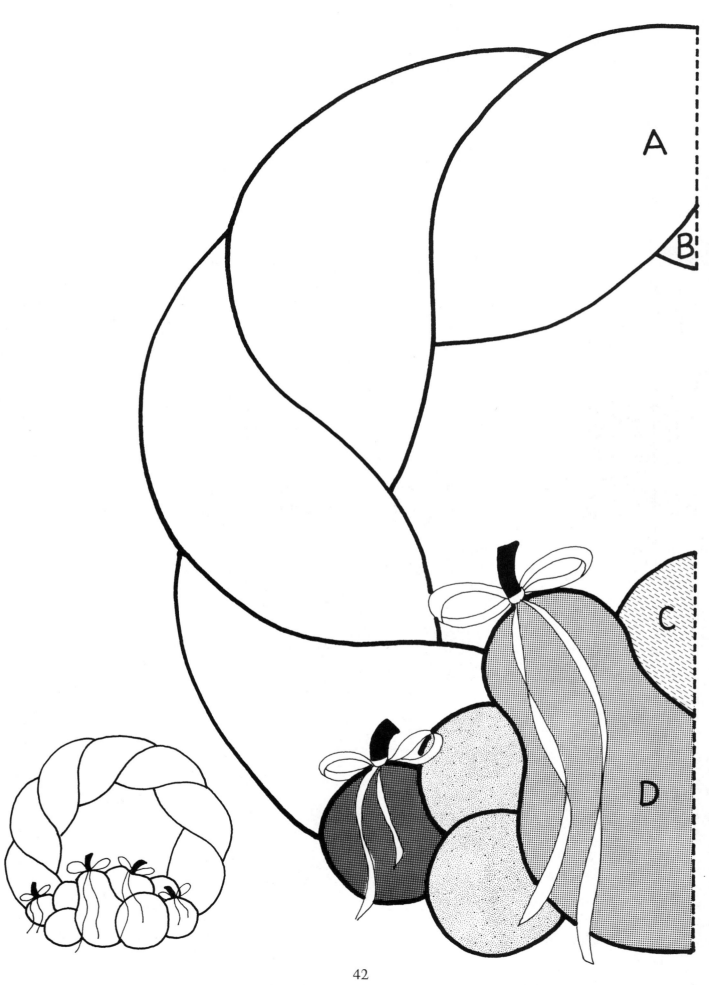

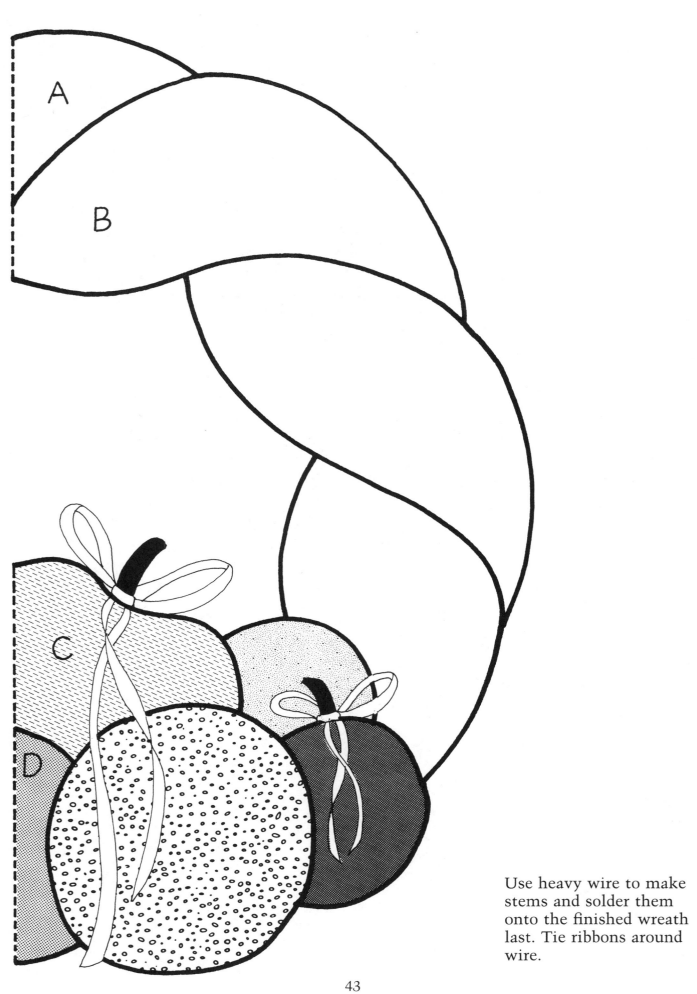

A

B

C

D

Use heavy wire to make stems and solder them onto the finished wreath last. Tie ribbons around wire.

A

B

C

44

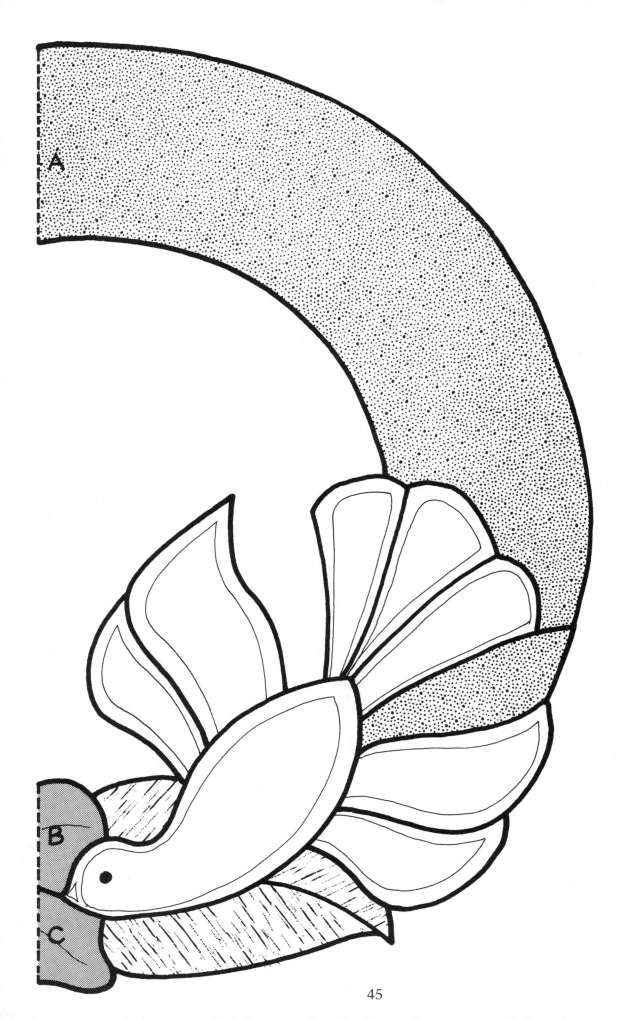

A

B

C

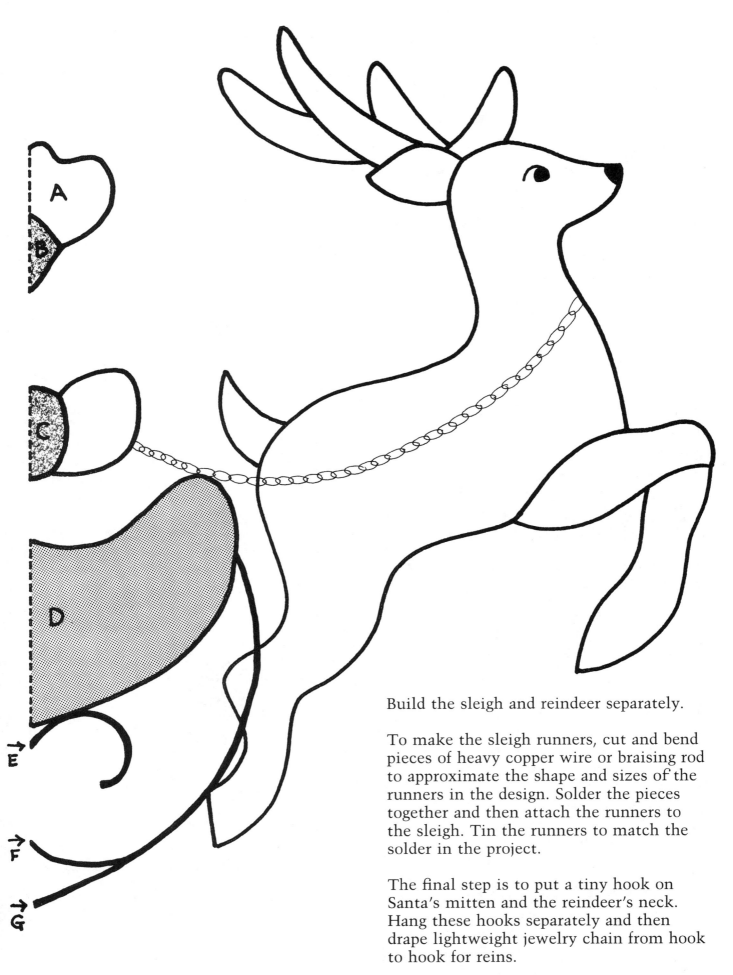

Build the sleigh and reindeer separately.

To make the sleigh runners, cut and bend pieces of heavy copper wire or braising rod to approximate the shape and sizes of the runners in the design. Solder the pieces together and then attach the runners to the sleigh. Tin the runners to match the solder in the project.

The final step is to put a tiny hook on Santa's mitten and the reindeer's neck. Hang these hooks separately and then drape lightweight jewelry chain from hook to hook for reins.

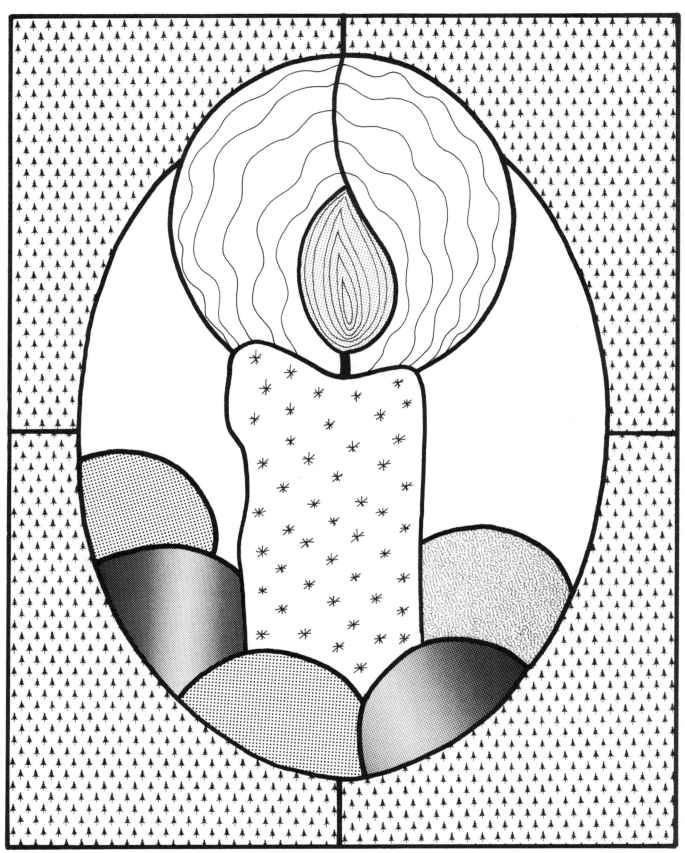

MINI-PANEL, WINDOW
OR MIRROR HANGING

Outer borders can be eliminated for small oval hanging piece.

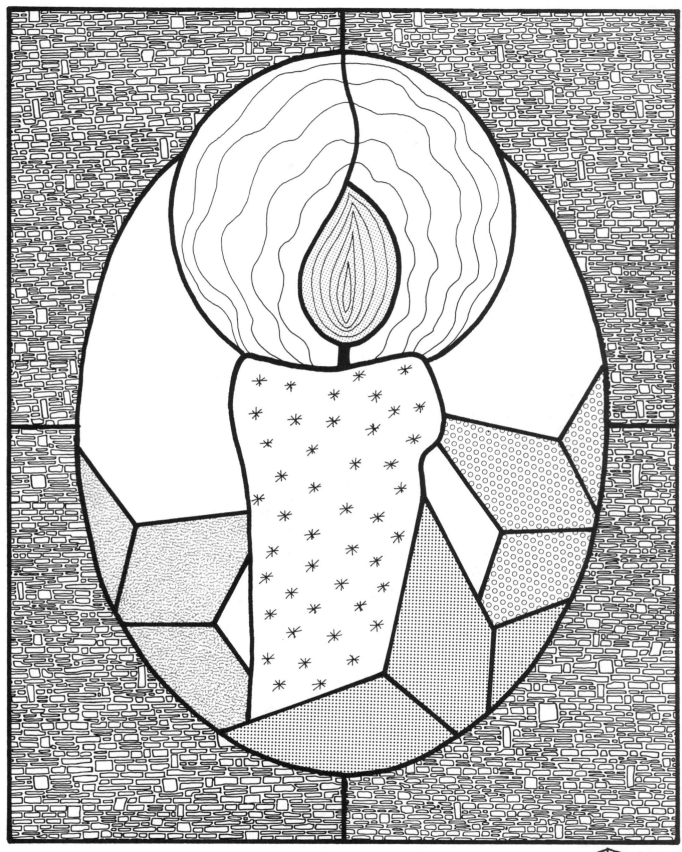

TABLE OR WINDOWSILL DECORATION

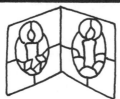

Hinge the two panels together and stand them up like a book.

PLANT ORNAMENTS

Solder different lengths of braising rod to the backs of several of these plant ornaments and decorate a plant by poking the rods deep into the soil.

For a free-swinging version, solder wire loops to the ends of braising rods and wire hooks to the tops of ornaments. Poke rods in the soil, then hang the ornaments on

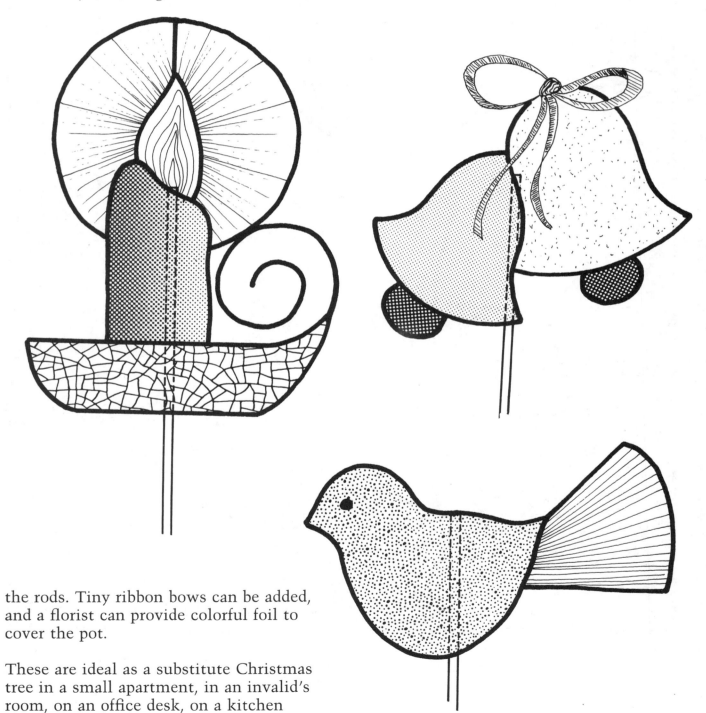

the rods. Tiny ribbon bows can be added, and a florist can provide colorful foil to cover the pot.

These are ideal as a substitute Christmas tree in a small apartment, in an invalid's room, on an office desk, on a kitchen counter, or for any other small area.

50

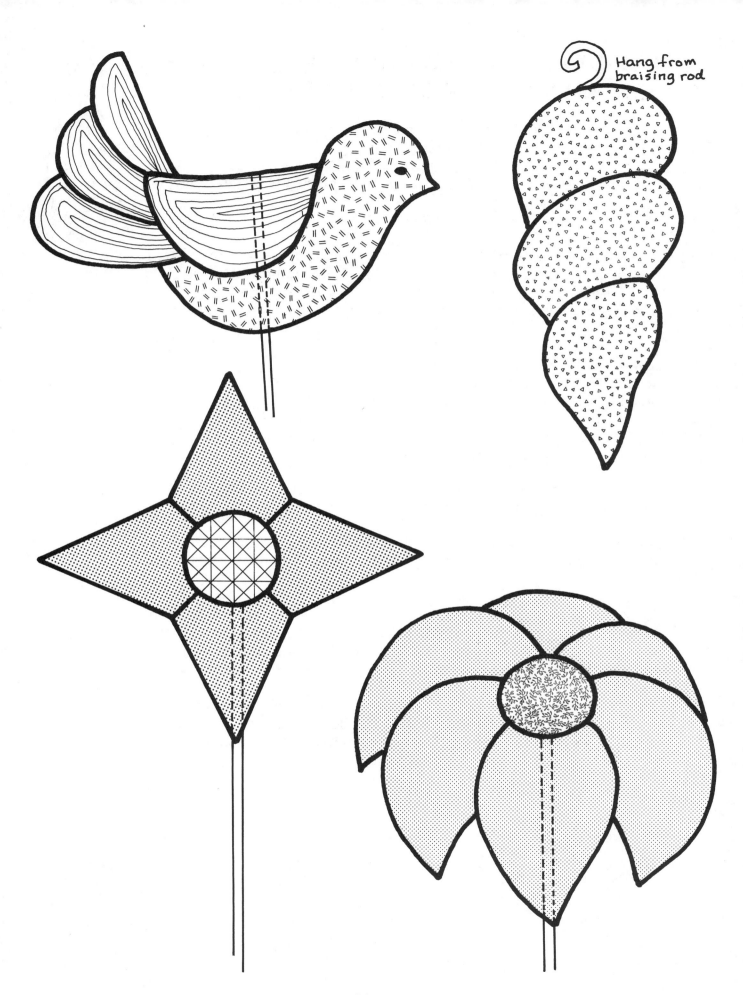

Hang from braising rod

51

THREE-DIMENSIONAL CHRISTMAS TREE OR TABLE, MANTLE, OR BUFFET CENTERPIECE

Yesterday mingles with today in this combination of nonperishable stained glass and wax candles from a bygone era.

1. First cut 7 pieces of glass from each pattern piece. (There are 5 layers.)

2. Copperfoil around each piece using 7/32-inch foil.

3. Lay the bottom section pieces edge to edge and secure them well with masking tape. Lift off of the table and form a standing ring. Secure the two end pieces together with masking tape. Tack solder the pieces, then completely solder all of the joints between each piece, inside and out.

4. Turn the bottom section upside down, with the scallops up. Tack a piece of lightweight copper wire all along the bottom edge for reinforcement. Then cover the entire wire with solder.

5. Bend 28 pieces of 2-inch-long wire at a 90-degree angle. (Use the template provided in the pattern.)

6. Repeat step 4 on the top side of the section, running reinforcing wire right over the top of each bent wire.

7. Construct the other 4 sections as described for the bottom section in steps 1 through 6. On the top section do not add the bent wires on top.

8. To assemble the tree, place the second section on the bottom section evenly, resting it on the bent wires with the points offset. Solder the two sections together. Continue adding sections one after the other, soldering them together as you go.

9. Using the tips of needle-nose pliers, bend the extending wires into small spirals to be used as candle holders. The larger size of birthday candles (available in the supermarket) are a good candle size to use for this tree.

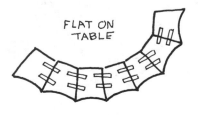
FLAT ON TABLE

TACK THEN SOLDER

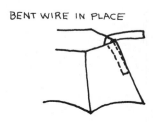
BENT WIRE IN PLACE

THREE-DIMENSIONAL CHRISTMAS TREE

10. Instead of candles, try other decorations for the tree. If the extending wires are looped, little glass balls can be hung from them, or tie small ribbon bows to them. Glass jewels or nuggets can be foiled and soldered to each wire. Tiny garlands or tinsel can be draped from wire to wire. Try a different decorating idea each year.

11. In decorating the top of the tree try another candle, a faceted jewel, or just leave it plain. A nativity scene backdrop to the tree is another idea.

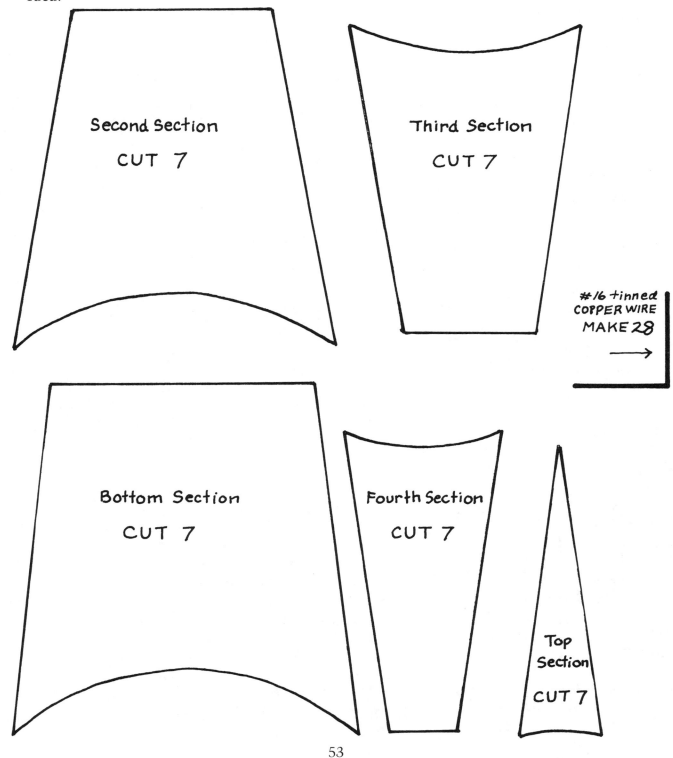

Second Section
CUT 7

Third Section
CUT 7

#16 tinned
COPPER WIRE
MAKE 28

Bottom Section
CUT 7

Fourth Section
CUT 7

Top Section
CUT 7

CHRISTMAS CANDLE COLLARS TABLE, MANTLE, OR BUFFET CENTERPIECE

These candle collars are fast and easy. They make great gifts any time of the year.

1. Use one of the patterns provided to cut 12 strips of glass.

2. Groze a tiny bit off each corner of each piece as shown on the pattern.

3. Stretch and cut two pieces of 1/4- or 3/16-inch U-channel lead about 14 inches long.

4. Stretch and cut 12 pieces of 1/4-inch H-channel lead the length of the glass strips, minus 1/2 inch if 1/4-inch U-channel lead is being used or minus 3/8 inch if 3/16-inch U-channel lead is being used.

Now you're ready to put it together.

5. On a workboard with a square raised corner, place one piece of the U lead along one of the raised edges as shown below. Slide the first piece of glass into the lead, butting the glass against the second raised edge of the board. Next place the first piece of H lead so that it is enclosed the long edge of the glass and butts against the U lead. It should be enough shorter than the glass so that later on the second U lead can slip all the way onto the end of the glass and barely touch the H lead.

6. Alternate all 12 glass and lead strips. Tap the sides and top gently as you go to insure a good fit. Block in one end securely.

7. Slide the second U-channel lead over the exposed ends of glass. It should just touch each of the H leads. If there are gaps, use solder to fill the ones that aren't too large. Or shift the H lead a bit to split the difference in large gaps between two joints.

8. Flux and solder all joints, using solder very sparingly. Do not let the solder dribble into the channels of the U lead on the end joints.

9. Use strips of masking tape to hold the left piece of glass in place. Remove the project from the workboard. With soldered joints facing to the inside, gently bend the assembly into a roughly circle shape.

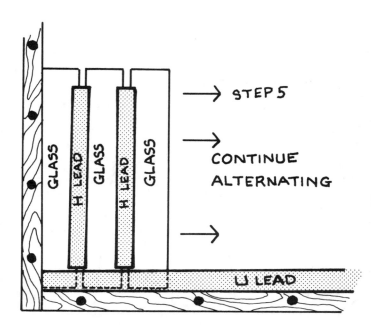

GLASS H LEAD GLASS H LEAD GLASS

→ STEP 5

→ CONTINUE ALTERNATING

→

U LEAD

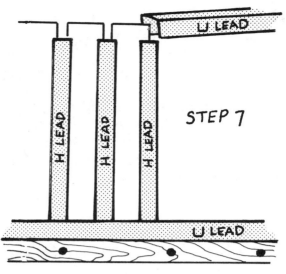

STEP 7

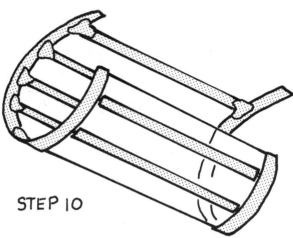

STEP 10

the interior surface. **Caution:** These would not be appropriate for holding food or any other consumable due to the danger of lead poisoning.

CUT 12 for 4¼" wide 9¼" tall project

Groze Corners

CUT 12 for 4¼" wide 7¼" tall project

Groze Corners

CUT 12 for 4¼" wide 5¼" tall project

Groze Corners

10. Bend the ends of U lead up and away from the glass, on both the top and the bottom of the assembly. Slip the remaining glass into the last H lead slot. Bend the U lead back down, trimming off excess to fit.

11. Tap the top and bottom to firmly seat the U lead onto the glass. Solder the outside joints. Adjust the bent shape to a good circle.

Variations: Any height, width, or number of glass strips can be used, although we do not recommend using fewer than 8. Oval shapes can be made. Bases can be soldered to the bottom for vessels such as pots and terrariums. To waterproof such a vessel, silicone sealer would have to be smeared liberally on

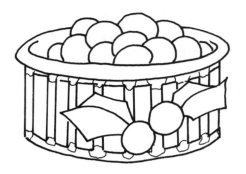

BOWL HOLDER TO SERVE CANDY, NUTS, FRUIT

It is tempting yet dangerous to serve food from beautiful stained glass. Foods, especially acid ones, pick up lead when they touch the lead strips or soldered lines, which are 50 percent lead. The dangers of lead poisoning are not worth the risk.

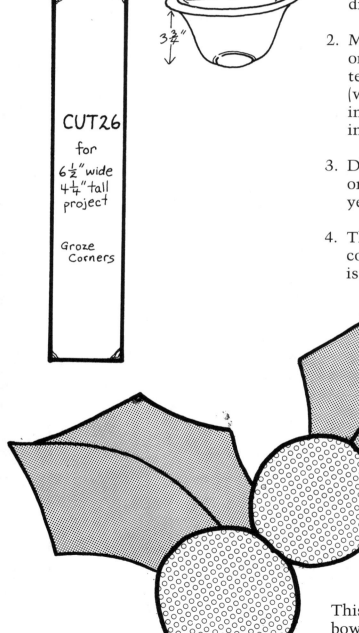

6"

3¾"

1. Purchase from a hardware or housewares store an ordinary oven-proof glass baking bowl, 6 inches in diameter, with a rim around the top as shown.

2. Make a "candle collar" following the procedures on pages 54 and 55, but use 26 strips of the pattern on this page, 3/16-inch U-channel lead (which will have to be longer than the 14 inches in the instructions on pages 54 and 55), and 3/16-inch H-channel lead also.

3. Decorate the bowl holder by soldering this holly or some other design in place, or leave it plain for year 'round serving.

4. The bowl sits on the holder with the bowl rim completely covering the top of the lead. The bowl is instantly removed for easy washing or refilling.

CUT 26

for

6½" wide
4¼" tall
project

Groze
Corners

This system can be adapted to any of the other glass bowls with rims on them that are commonly available. Adjust the size by changing the number of strips and their width and height.

BASES FOR STANDING FIGURES AND TABLE DECORATIONS

Method 1

Use the following method for Christmas Village and Nativity Scenes (pages 58 through 67).

1. Cut a 2-piece base of clear glass as shown on the right. Each piece should be 1 inch wide and at least as long as the bottom of the figure. Round each outside corner. Foil and solder the pieces together.

2. Center the figure vertically on the base and solder it in place front and back.

Method 2

1. Cut the base from mirror or clear glass. Make it the length of the bottom of the project and 2 or more inches wide.

2. Foil all around and solder the project to the base at about 85 degrees. (Tip the project very slightly toward the base.) Test the project and base for strength. Very tall projects may need to be braces with one or more pieces of heavy wire.

3. Holders for tapered candles: Buy copper pipe caps at a hardware store. These are inexpensive and come in ¼, ½, and ¾-inch diameters and larger. Choose the candle style that will look best with the project and buy the cap size accordingly. To attach the caps, flux the bottom of each cap and the edge of the glass where they will be attached. Hold the cap with needle-nose pliers and heat the bottom well with a soldering iron. When the bottom of the cap is hot, solder it in place on the base.

For an alternate method of making projects, stand (using tube hinges) see *Christmas in Stained Glass, Book I* (Hidden House Publications), page 7.

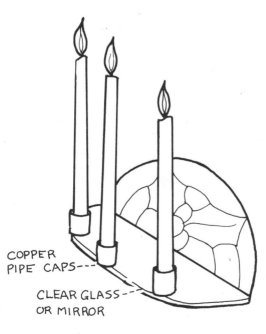

COPPER PIPE CAPS---

CLEAR GLASS---
OR MIRROR

CHRISTMAS VILLAGE SCENE

See page 57 for instructions on
how to make the figures stand
by themselves.

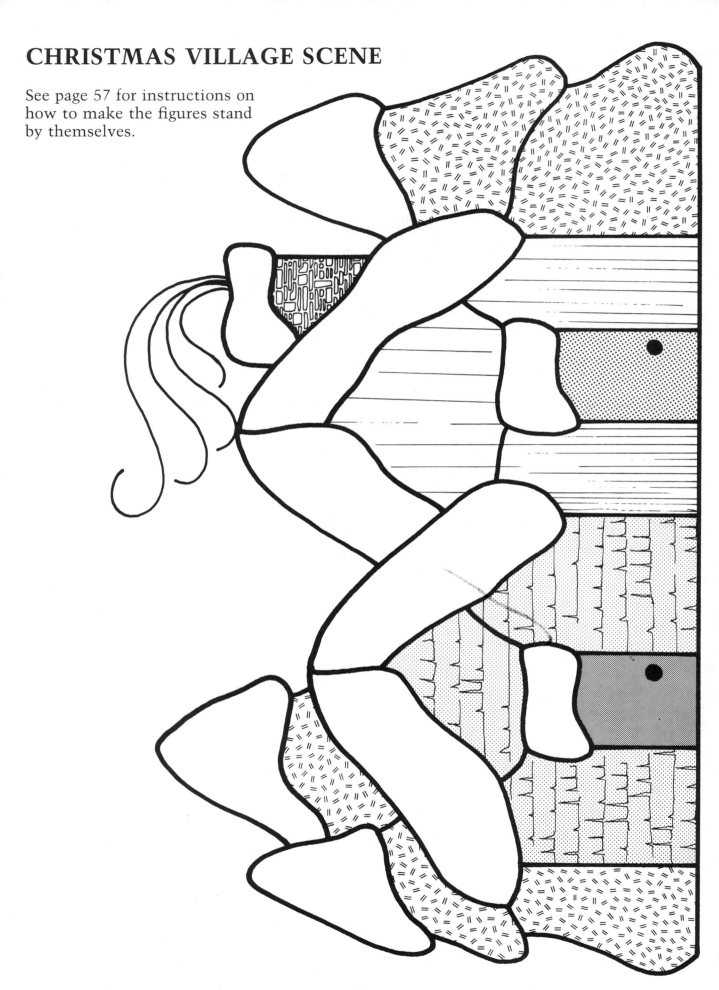

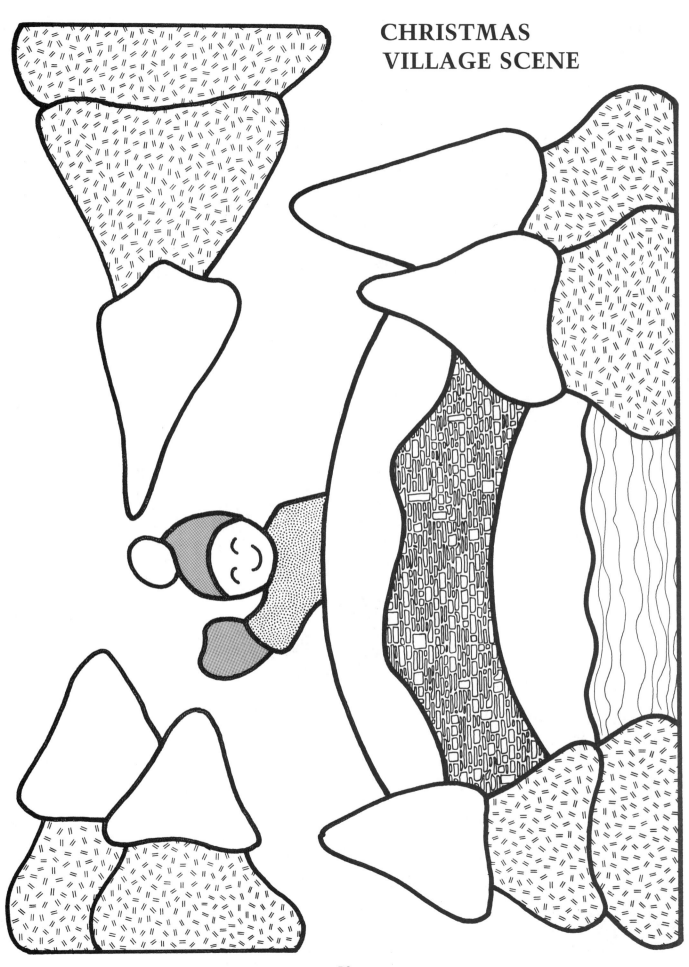

CHRISTMAS
VILLAGE SCENE

CHRISTMAS VILLAGE SCENE

See page 57 for instructions on how to make the figures stand by themselves.

It isn't necessary to make all of the parts of the village. Several of the figures would be fine as individual projects. Or, group just two or three figures on a piece of mirror glass to create a table centerpiece.

Suggested groupings:
- Carolers and streetlight
- Church and houses
- Bridge scene with children
- Snowman, single girl, and animals

These would be excellent when surrounded by "angel hair" and twinkle lights.

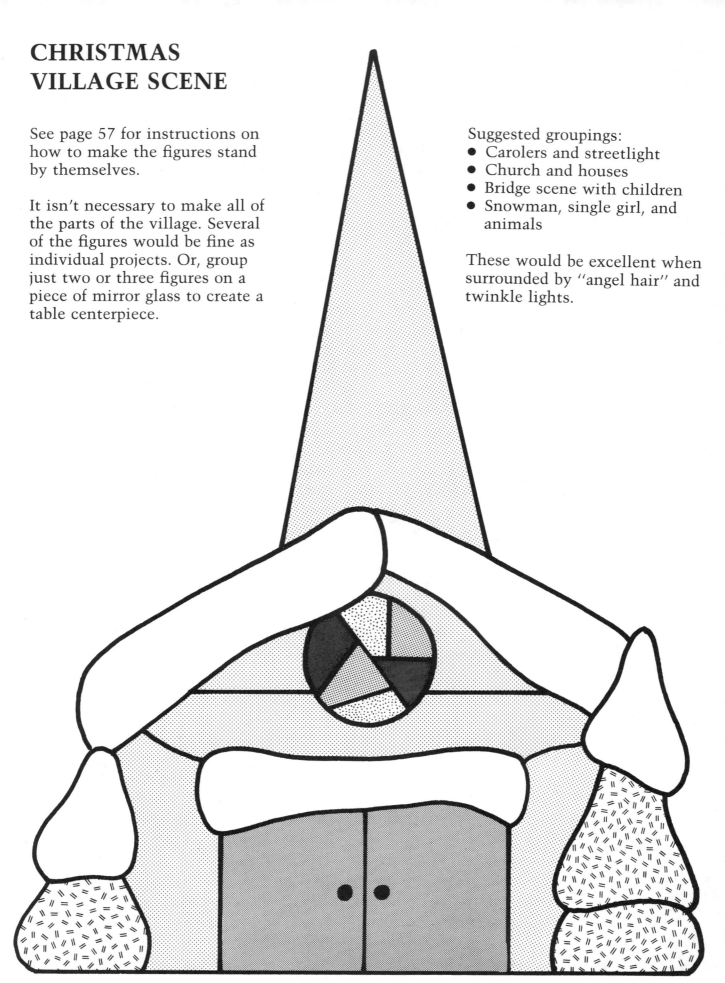

CHRISTMAS VILLAGE SCENE

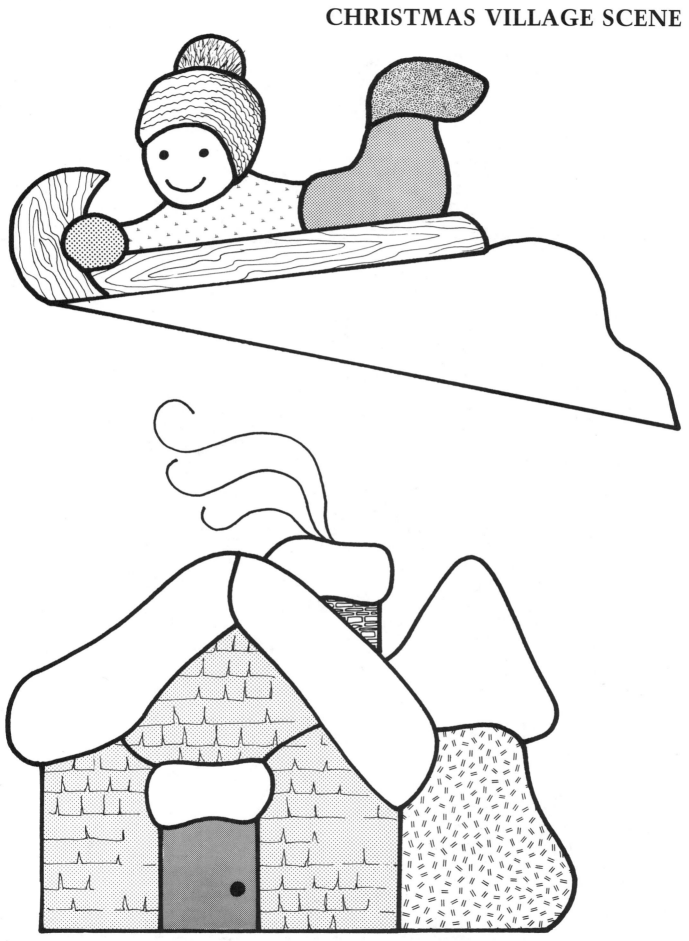

CHRISTMAS VILLAGE SCENE

CHRISTMAS VILLAGE SCENE

See page 57 for instructions on how to make
the figures stand by themselves.

NATIVITY SCENE

See page 57 for instructions on how to make
the figures stand by themselves.

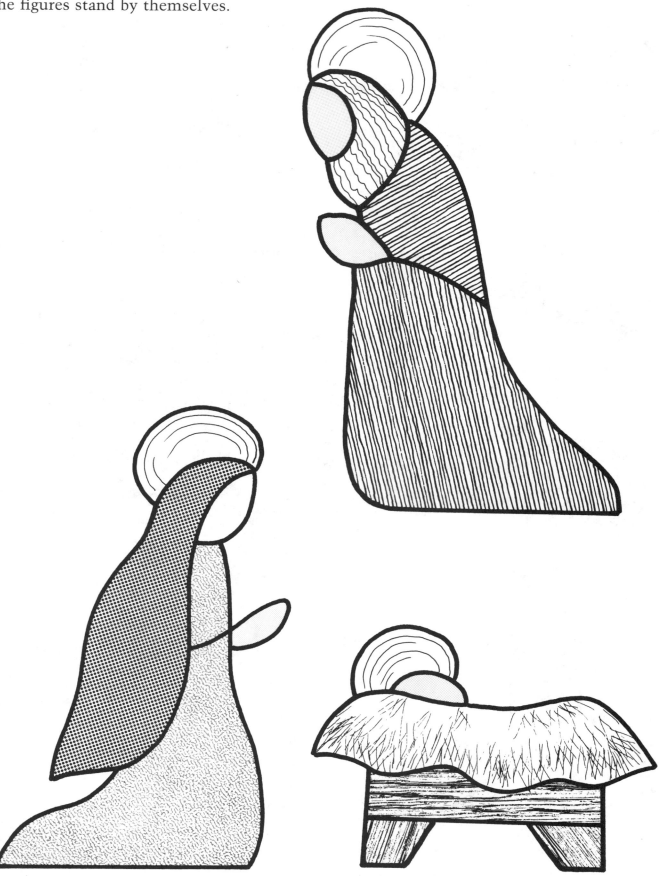

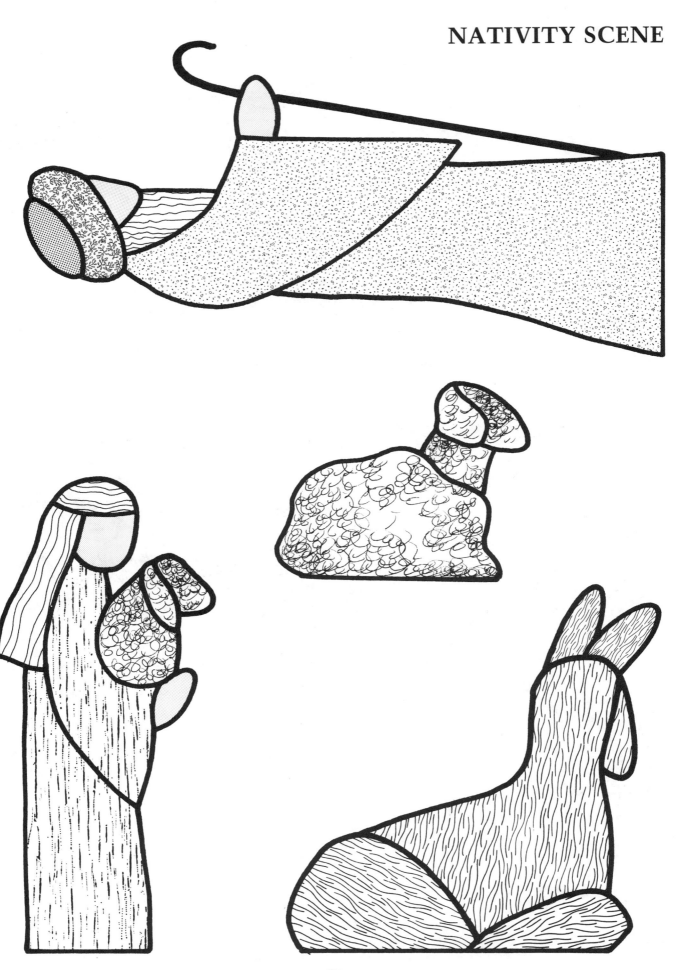

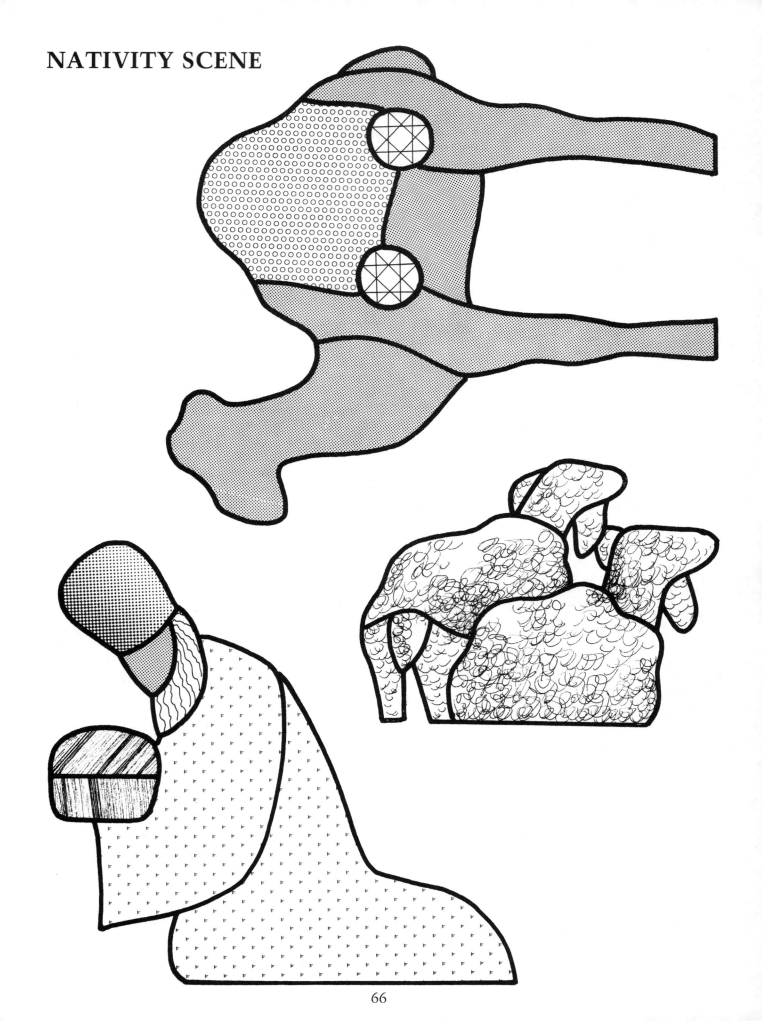

NATIVITY SCENE

It isn't necessary to make all of the parts of the nativity scene. Several of the pieces would make nice groupings for tabletop decorations, with or without the three-piece backdrop.

Suggested groupings are
- Baby Jesus, Mary, and Joseph
- Three Wise Men and camel
- Baby Jesus, sheperds, and sheep

See page 57 for instructions on how to make the figures stand by themselves.

NATIVITY SCENE BACKDROP

(right and left sections)

Make two sets, Use mirror or stained glass for the center area. Stained glass can be substituted for jewels.

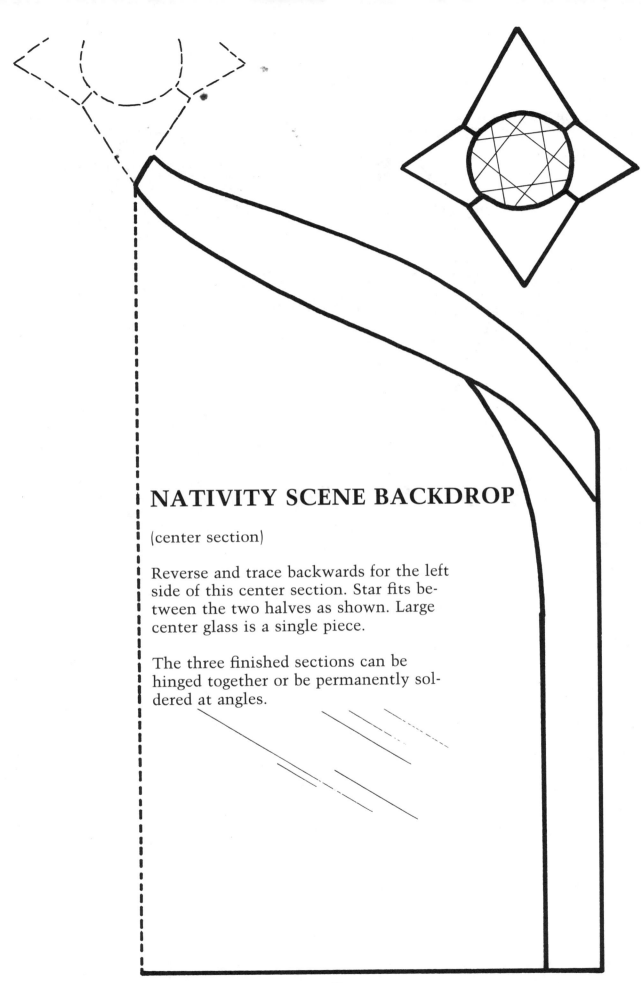

NATIVITY SCENE BACKDROP

(center section)

Reverse and trace backwards for the left side of this center section. Star fits between the two halves as shown. Large center glass is a single piece.

The three finished sections can be hinged together or be permanently soldered at angles.

WINDOW OR MIRROR HANGING

Build and hang parts separately. Join the parts with lightweight chain to represent an airplane pulling a sign through the air. Paint letters using glass paints or acrylics in your own lettering style.

WINDOW OR MIRROR HANGING, TABLE DECORATION

Follow the dotted line to make a table decoration. See pages 26 and 57 for ways to make the project stand by itself. Decorate with several colors of curly ribbon after the project is completed. The tabletop version could be surrounded by confetti for an attractive effect.